Orca Origins

Nikki Tate & Dani Tate-Stratton

BIRTHDAYS

Beyond Cake and Ice Cream

ORCA BOOK PUBLISHERS

Library and Archives Canada Cataloguing in Publication

Tate, Nikki, 1962–, author
Birthdays: beyond cake and ice cream / Nikki Tate and Dani Tate-Stratton.
(Orca origins)

Includes index.

Issued in print and electronic formats.
ISBN 978-1-4598-1297-0 (hardback).—ISBN 978-1-4598-1298-7 (pdf).— ISBN 978-1-4598-1299-4 (epub)

1. Birthdays—Juvenile literature. I. Tate-Stratton, Danielle, 1987–, author II. Title.
GT2430.T38 2017   j394.2   c2016-904488-2
c2016-904489-0

First published in the United States, 2017
Library of Congress Control Number: 2016949042

Summary: Part of the nonfiction Orca Origins series for middle readers. Illustrated with color photographs, this book covers the history of modern celebrations and discusses the many birthday traditions around the world.

Orca Book Publishers is dedicated to preserving the environment and has printed this book on Forest Stewardship Council® certified paper.

Orca Book Publishers gratefully acknowledges the support for its publishing programs provided by the following agencies: the Government of Canada through the Canada Book Fund and the Canada Council for the Arts, and the Province of British Columbia through the BC Arts Council and the Book Publishing Tax Credit.

Design by Rachel Page
Front cover photos by Shutterstock.com, iStock.com, William Steen
Back cover photo by iStock.com
Author photo: Nichole Taylor Photography

ORCA BOOK PUBLISHERS
www.orcabook.com

Printed and bound in Canada.

20 19 18 17 • 4 3 2 1

CONTENTS

Chapter Three:
Milestone Birthdays

Candles add the perfect finishing touch to any birthday cake.
iStock.com

Blow out your candles and make a wish for the upcoming year. Remember to keep your wish a secret!
Getty Images

Introduction

In our family, birthdays have always been eagerly anticipated and considered to be a great reason to celebrate. We've lived, studied and traveled in many countries, and our relatives come from Germany, the United Kingdom, Japan, Sweden and Italy. Over the years we've enjoyed borrowing birthday traditions from many different places and had a lot of fun inventing ways to celebrate that are unique to our family. A few years ago, my daughter Dani organized a memorable surprise birthday party for me. With so many friends and family gathered in one place, it was inevitable that we shared memories of other birthdays. We talked about birthday camping trips, the year we held a murder mystery party, and the time there were pony rides. We've stayed up late watching movies at sleepover parties, played classic North American games like Pin the

Nikki's fifth birthday party featured pony rides for all the guests.

Helga Williams

7

Dani attended a friend's fourth birthday party that had a country and western theme, complete with costumes.

Helga Williams

Tail on the Donkey, Hot Potato and Pass the Parcel, and feasted on treats like cake, ice cream, hot dogs and potato chips. I love to dress up in costumes and have been known to show up at parties dressed as a pirate, a fairy or a clown.

Memories of fabulous past parties were a source of inspiration for this book. We wondered if birthdays affect other families in the same way. How much does where you grow up influence the way you celebrate getting a year older? Have people always celebrated birthdays? The more we investigated, the more we learned there's a lot more to birthdays than cake, presents, a few games and perhaps a goody bag. We discovered there are as many ways to observe birthdays around the world as there are places in which to do it. We found birthdays involving bullet ants, red eggs, flour throwing, door knob polishing and horse racing! Maybe next year we'll be asking our friends to wish us *saeng-il chukha hae* (Happy Birthday) over bowls of *miyeok-guk* (seaweed soup)! How will you celebrate the start of your next year on Earth?

Papel picado (cut paper) banners indicate a celebration, such as a birthday, is in progress. *AugustineChang/iStock.com*

An example at the Kom Ombo Temple of an early Egyptian calendar carved in stone.
Zhaojiankang/Dreamstime.com

ONE

THE BIRTH OF BIRTHDAYS

It's impossible to know exactly when people first started to celebrate birthdays. At some point in the Bronze Age (between about 3300 BCE and 1000 BCE), people started keeping track of time using calendars. Before that it would have been hard to pinpoint what day of the year a baby was born. Imagine not knowing exactly when to have your birthday party! While people knew roughly what time of year water froze and thawed or when it was time to sow and harvest crops, in ancient times the lack of a consistent calendar made it tough to keep track of important dates.

Party Like An Egyptian

Though scholars are still debating the exact date calendars began to be used, it's thought that the Ancient Egyptians

Someone who is born on February 29 during a leap year is called a **leaper** or a **leapling**. In non-leap years, leaplings celebrate on either February 28 or March 1.

This ceiling in the Abydos Temple in Egypt shows early Egyptian astrological symbols.
AmandaLewis/iStock.com

were among the first people to use one, about 5,000 years ago. The Ancient Egyptian calendar had twelve months, each of which had 30 days. It takes the Earth 365 days to travel once around the sun, so the Ancient Egyptians didn't have quite enough days to add up to a full year (12 x 30 = 360). They added an extra day (known as *epagomenae*) to five of the months. Those spare days became feast days to commemorate the birthdays of Egyptian gods. The first day of each new year was said to be Ra-Horakhty's birthday. Ra-Horakhty was the god of the sun in Ancient Egypt.

Egyptian kings were called **pharaohs** and were believed to become godlike once they were elevated to the status of pharaoh. Egyptians kept careful track of the positions and movements of stars and planets on their pharaohs' birthdays; taking note of where heavenly bodies are at a given point in time is an important aspect of the practice of **astrology**. The Ancient Egyptians believed that the astrological readings of these living gods could affect harvests and other important aspects of life. When the pharaohs' birthdays occurred, the whole community contributed to the occasion, often closing businesses for days at a time as they prepared huge feasts in honor of the important date.

The date of a pharaoh's **coronation** was also thought of as a kind of birthday because crowning a pharaoh elevated him to a new status. Thousands of years after the death of Pharoah Ramses II in 1213 BCE, the people of Egypt still celebrate both his birthday and the date of his coronation. At Abu Simbel, one of the many monuments he ordered to have built in his name, there is an inner sanctum that is normally shrouded in darkness. However, on two days of the year (the dates traditionally

A coronation, such as the one shown here, was considered to be like a pharaoh's birthday.
Passion Images/Shutterstock.com

The Great Temple at Abu Simbel contains an inner sanctum illuminated by the sun only on Ramses II's two birthdays.
Emanuele Mazzoni Photo/Shutterstock.com

On her eighth birthday, the child actress Shirley Temple received thousands of cards and gifts from fans around the world, including a baby kangaroo from Australia.

recognized as Ramses II's birthday and coronation), the sun is aligned perfectly so it illuminates the statues of the gods and goddesses inside. Because the solar calendar shifts a little from year to year and the temple was moved to a slightly different location to protect it from erosion (slow deterioration over time caused by wind and rain), these dates of illumination are not the same as they would have been in 1200 BCE. That doesn't matter to the thousands of visitors who come to take in the spectacle each year and remember the early birthday of a king-god.

Astrology was also important in the world of Ancient China, though it was the year of birth and not the month that was considered most significant. In China, the signs of the zodiac change annually. Each year is represented by a different animal. The cycle repeats every twelve years.

Each year of the Chinese Zodiac is represented by a different animal.
Jasmineforum/Dreamstime.com

The first recorded birthday gathering is noted in the book of Genesis in the Old Testament. An Egyptian pharaoh is described as celebrating a birthday: "And it came to pass the third day, which was Pharaoh's birthday, that he made a feast unto all his servants" (King James Version, Genesis 40:20–22). Today, it's common to observe a birthday by sharing food and festivities with friends and family, in a spirit of sharing like that of the pharaoh and his servants.

When in Rome

In other ancient civilizations special festivities were sometimes held on the day a baby was born but not necessarily each year after that. The Roman emperor Caligula held two days of horse racing to commemorate the birth of his daughter Drusilla. The emperor's over-the-top celebrations were held in part because he believed himself to be a god. To his way of thinking, Drusilla was the child of a god and that meant her arrival deserved special attention.

The birth of any baby in Ancient Rome was considered to be an important occasion worthy of a lengthy celebration, though not as lavish as Drusilla's. Unfortunately, because health care wasn't as good then as it is now, many infants died in the first week of life. *Dies lustricus*, or the "day of purification," was a momentous occasion held eight or nine days after the birth. Families waited for this period of time to pass before they fully welcomed a new baby into the family. Several rituals were performed. In one, fathers raised the babies from the ground to the sky to show that they took responsibility as the father. This was also the day when newborns were given a name.

Birthday Treats

The Story of the Chinese Zodiac

In one traditional version of the Chinese zodiac story, the emperor invited twelve animals to gather for a feast. The order in which they arrived is the order used for the zodiac signs, though the fastest was not the winner of this race. The rat hitched a ride on the ox and at the last moment scampered down the ox's head and stretched his neck out. He arrived a nose ahead of his transportation system, which is why the Chinese zodiac cycle always begins with the rat—not the speediest animal, but possibly the sneakiest. According to the story, the mighty dragon should have arrived first, but he kept getting distracted by doing good deeds along the way.

You might have noticed there's no cat in the Chinese zodiac. Once again, the rat was a troublemaker! The cat was invited to the party, but before starting the race, he decided he needed a nap. Foolishly, he asked the rat to wake him up when the race to the emperor's palace began. Rat "forgot" and the cat slept through everything. Ever since, rats and cats haven't liked each other much!

Birthday Treats

Who Was Artemis?

The Greeks honored many gods whose home, it was said, was atop Mount Olympus. Zeus was the ruler of the Olympian gods and the father of many children, including the twins Artemis and Apollo. Artemis was one of three goddesses (along with Selene and Hecate) associated with the moon. Artemis's birthday was observed on the sixth day of the eleventh month (known then as Thargelion). Ancient Greeks celebrated Apollo's birthday a day later on the seventh day of the eleventh month.

The Greek goddess Artemis.
Gors4730/Dreamstime.com

The Ancient Romans are thought to have been the first to mark the birthdays of people from all walks of life, as opposed to only gods or important leaders. However, only birthdays of males were observed and, at first, only the head of the household was entitled to this honor. Women and girls were out of luck until about the twelfth century, when, finally, both genders took note of birthdays. Even then, wealthy and powerful people were much more likely to celebrate birthdays than people living ordinary lives.

Ancient Greek Birthday Festivals

The Ancient Greeks are said to have taken the idea of celebrating birthdays from the Egyptians. In the same way that people living by the Nile River celebrated the birthdays of their pharaohs rather than mere mortals, Grecian festivities often honored Greek gods and goddesses. These festivals were held on specific days of the month and incorporated certain rituals, which changed depending on the god or goddess being feted. When the time came to pay respect to the moon goddess Artemis, Greeks gave sacrifices of sweet moon-shaped cakes intended to celebrate her radiance. Burning candles on top of the cakes represented the glow of the moon. They were the very first birthday candles and also served a second purpose: the Ancient Greeks believed that, as the smoke rose from the candles toward the sky, prayers were carried to the gods and goddesses above. Today's practice of making a wish when we blow out our candles may have originated with this tradition.

The Early Middle Ages

During the Early Middle Ages (between about 500 and 1500 CE) individual birthdays were frowned upon as the power of the Christian faith spread and such festivities were seen as belonging to **pagan** (non-Christian) traditions. In the Bible, the main religious text of the Christian faith, there are no references to ordinary citizens observing birthdays, so in the early days of Christianity only the birth of Jesus Christ was recognized. Though there is some disagreement about the actual date of Jesus's birth, most Christians celebrate it on December 25.

In the Catholic tradition certain individuals who behave in a particularly holy way are identified as saints. Special days were named after each saint to commemorate the day the saint died. Because death was considered to be the time when one entered heaven (sometimes thought of as being born into a new life), the saints' days were thought of as birthdays.

This nativity scene depicts the birth of Jesus, one of history's most famous birthdays. *Shutterstock.com*

The Cathedral of Saint Sava in Belgrade, Serbia, is one of the ten largest church buildings in the world, and one place where Serbians come to honor saints on their special days.
Reddiplomat/iStock.com

Eventually, every day of the year was named after a saint, and people applauded the good deeds and holy behavior of the saints by holding a celebration. Many people shared names with the saints, and a tradition began that anyone who had the same name as a saint could celebrate on the saint's feast day. These **name days** were similar in some ways to birthdays in that they were associated with gift-giving, special greetings and good wishes, and visiting with friends and family. In some countries, name days are also celebrated today.

Not all modern Christian traditions celebrate birthdays. Jehovah's Witnesses, for example, do not celebrate individual birthdays as they believe that, since birthdays are not discussed in the Bible, they should not be recognized as important events. Instead, Jehovah's Witnesses emphasize giving over receiving and suggest that gifts and treats should be shared throughout the year and not on any one particular day.

What Day Is It?

Sometimes, the day of the week on which a baby was born holds a special significance. In Ghana, one of a child's several names may be based on the day of the week they were born on. In the Twi language (a tribal language spoken in Ghana), a male child born on a Thursday may have Yao as part of his name or a girl born on the same day may include Yaa as part of hers.

You may be familiar with the old nursery rhyme, "Monday's Child." One version of the rhyme goes like this:

A child like this one in Accra, Ghana, may have been named after the day of the week on which it was born.
Anton_Ivanov/Shutterstock.com

Give It a Whirl!

Back to the Future

On your next birthday, take a few minutes to do the following:

1. Think about how the past year was for you. What was the best thing that happened to you? The worst? What was one important thing you learned over the previous year?

2. Record your thoughts in a journal or notebook or on an electronic device. Next year, look back at what you wrote and ask yourself the same questions. Don't throw away each year's reflections. They will become a wonderful peek into your childhood many years from now.

3. Set a goal for next year. Write down your goal, and seal it in an envelope. Next year, open the envelope and see whether you were successful in reaching your goal.

Monday's child is fair of face
Tuesday's child is full of grace
Wednesday's child is full of woe
Thursday's child has far to go
Friday's child is loving and giving
Saturday's child works hard for a living
But the child who is born on the Sabbath day
Is fair and wise and good in every way.

Do you know what day of the week you were born on? Do you think the rhyme accurately reflects your life or personality?

Birthday Treats

The Hudson's Bay Company

When we first moved to Canada from Australia in 1969, my family and I soon learned there were a few things that all Canadians knew about. One of them was the Hudson's Bay Company. Founded on May 2, 1670, the company began life as a series of trading posts across the country and later became a department store. On May 2, 1970, the Bay celebrated its three-hundredth birthday. Anyone in Canada who shared the company's birth date was invited to a big party at a local Bay store. We made a special road trip from Banff (where we lived) to Calgary, a hundred kilometers (sixty-two miles) away (where the nearest party was being held) so I could attend the gala affair with several hundred other people. That party, with a huge cake and decorations and a *lot* of people singing "Happy Birthday," made an impression I'll never forget! —NT

Hudson's Bay Company stores across Canada, like this one in Manitoba, threw a huge party for the company's three-hundredth anniversary.
Archives of Manitoba

The Renaissance

Toy tin soldiers such as these from the eighteenth century were some of the first mass-produced toys popular as birthday gifts.
Fedor Selivanov/Shutterstock.com

During the **Renaissance** (a time of cultural rebirth that took place in Europe between about 1300 and 1700 CE), the churches maintained records of births, deaths and marriages, though birth dates were not always very accurate. Sometimes, only the date of a **baptism** was recorded, and since baptisms can happen anytime after a baby is born, it's hard to know the exact date of birth.

In England, accurate records were not mandatory for births until the mid-1800s and in the United States, not until after 1900. Perhaps it was this shift in paying attention to the date of birth that also led to more attention being paid to someone's birthday each year.

Each year Americans spend between seven and eight billion dollars on greeting cards. The nearly two billion birthday cards bought and shared represent nearly 60 percent of all cards sent each year in the United States.

Omi's Apple Cake

Nikki's German grandmother was a wonderful baker. Family birthdays always feature this delicious cake.

Ingredients

4-5 medium apples
2 eggs
¾ cup vegetable oil
2 cups sugar
2 cups flour
2 teaspoons cinnamon
1 teaspoon baking soda
½ teaspoon salt
⅓ cup water
1 teaspoon vanilla

Directions

Preheat oven to 350°F. Grease the bottom of a 10-inch round springform pan. Peel the apples and cut into small cubes. You will end up with approximately 4 cups of chopped apples. Set aside. In a large bowl, mix eggs and oil together until smooth. Add all remaining ingredients except apples and stir until well combined. Fold in apples. The batter will be very thick. Pour into cake pan and pat down with a spatula or wooden spoon to spread evenly. Bake for 45–55 minutes, or until a toothpick inserted in the center comes out clean. Cool in pan for 20 minutes, then release the springform and remove the ring. Leave the cake on the bottom of the pan until fully cooled, then enjoy.

The Industrial Revolution

The **Industrial Revolution**, was the period of time starting in the mid-1700s and lasting about a hundred years. During this time the invention of machines and the automation of manufacturing made many aspects of life much easier. Lots of people moved from the countryside to cities, where they found work in factories. How people celebrated birthdays was affected by these changes. For example, as more goods were mass produced and became widely distributed due to the invention of railways, the cost of many items, including baked goods like cakes, plummeted and became affordable for more families. Manufactured toys like jigsaw puzzles, tin soldiers and dolls, which had traditionally been made by hand, became popular with families that earned enough money to buy such items as birthday presents.

Good Times or Sad?

Though birthdays are often considered to be a reason to celebrate, this hasn't always been the case. It is believed that long ago Jewish people thought of birthdays as being sad reminders that the end of one's life was getting closer. Today, many Jewish families believe a birthday is a day to acknowledge one's good fortune in having been born. A birthday is a chance to look back on the previous year and consider both the good and not-so-good things that happened. Jews are encouraged to give a little more to charity and to spend extra time praying on their birthdays.

The tradition of wearing a paper crown on your birthday goes back to the days when only kings and queens celebrated their birthdays. When members of a royal family celebrated, it was a chance to wear their crowns for a day.

Jawaharlal Nehru, a very important figure in Indian history, is honored here with a sculpture depicting him surrounded by children. His birthday is marked annually in India by Children's Day.
Viacheslav Belyaev/Dreamstime.com

Birthday Treats

Unregistered Births

According to the United Nations International Children's Emergency Fund (UNICEF), the birth of about one of every three babies is never registered. In some countries, mothers give birth at home, and sometimes those homes are far away from hospitals or clinics where the birth registration process is automatic. If the registration process is expensive or not well understood by adults with very little education, parents may not register their children. The implications of not knowing your birth date are much bigger than just missing out on a party every year. If a child's birth is not registered, it's not always possible to keep track of whether the child has received proper health care or vaccinations, or when he or she should start school. Later in life, not having a birth certificate may make it difficult or impossible to obtain a driver's license, vote in elections or apply for a passport.

Big Birthday Bashes—Commemorating History

Sometimes, celebrating the birthday of a famous person is a way to commemorate significant historical events. In some cases, these festivities are held on the exact day of the person's birth. In India, November 14 is the date of Jawaharlal Nehru's birthday. Nehru was India's first prime minister, leading the nation from 1947 to 1964. He believed strongly in the education and well-being of children, which is why the national holiday celebrated in his honor is called *Bal Divas*, or Children's Day.

However, national holidays and celebrations can also be held on a consistent day of the week close to the birthday of the person being remembered. In the United States, Martin Luther King Day is held on the third Monday of January, close to his birth date of January 15. In Canada, Queen Victoria's birthday (also called Fête de la Reine) is always held on the last Monday before May 25, Queen Victoria's actual date of birth.

According to traditional texts, Buddha was born in about 563 BCE in what is now known as Nepal. Buddha's birthday is marked in different ways depending on location and the particular type of Buddhism being practiced. The date on which Buddha's birthday falls changes slightly each year, but generally takes place sometime in April or May.

From not being celebrated at all to having nearly everyone acknowledge the passing of another year, birthdays have changed over time. Read on to find out how people in different parts of the world like to observe this special event.

In South Korea, lotus lanterns decorate temples during the month of Buddha's birthday. *hanhanpeggy/iStock.com*

Friends look on as this blindfolded partygoer tries to break open a piñata and release candy and small toys for everyone to share.
Getty Images

TWO

CELEBRATING BIRTHDAYS AROUND THE WORLD

People celebrate the anniversary of their birth in many different ways. The special food, songs, games, decorations and outfits that characterize birthdays vary from place to place, as do the ways in which people decide how old someone is. If you are planning a party, you might want to borrow traditions from other parts of the world to make your next birthday extra special.

Keeping Track of Birthdays

No matter where you live, it's helpful to know whose birthday is coming up. Birthday books and calendars are one way to keep track of when birthdays of friends and family members are approaching. In the Netherlands,

> The Asante people of Ghana call their birthday a soul day. Special washing rituals, feasting and wearing white clothing are all part of the festivities.

birthday calendars are often found hanging in the bathroom. In many countries, it's common to record birthdays in a special book or in an app. Birthday calendars are different from regular calendars because they don't include the days of the week. Each date falls on a different day of the week from year to year, so these calendars include only the dates and plenty of space to add the names of those celebrating their special days. That means such calendars can be used for many years. Popular social media sites like Facebook, which sends out birthday reminders automatically, make it easy to remember to send a special greeting on someone's birthday.

Birthday Treats

Birthday Calendars

Birthday calendars like the one pictured below help us to remember the dates of each birthday in the family. As children are born, their names are easily added to the relevant month. When I got married a couple of years ago, adding my husband's family to the calendar helped me keep all of the new dates straight! —DTS

Who's on the Guest List?

In some places, only a few people close to the person whose birthday is being celebrated are invited to the party.

This wooden birthday calendar has rings to allow the addition of new people and dates.
Dani Tate-Stratton/skog.ca

That's certainly not the case with the Winnebago tribe in the United States, where parties are big and anyone can come join the fun. News of the party is spread by word of mouth. Winnebago birthday parties start in the evening and can last all night. Part of the fun is to try to provide the birthday person with all their favorite kinds of food. Because so many people attend parties like these, the cake has to be big enough for everyone to have a piece. A sheet cake (a large slab of cake that can be cut into lots of pieces) is carried around so all the guests have a chance to see it before it's cut. It's considered a great honor to be asked to cut the cake. Drumming and singing take place throughout the evening. Sometimes adults play a game with the children in which the adult holds a bone or stone in one hand and then the children must guess where it's hidden.

Nigeria is another place where a huge party may be held on someone's birthday. Sometimes a whole goat is prepared, so there is plenty of tasty food to go around. Jollof rice (rice with tomatoes, tomato paste, onions, and spices) is a popular West African dish that might be served at a party or celebration.

A sheet cake similar to one the Winnebago tribe would have at their birthday celebrations.
Alphababy/Dreamstime.com

Invitations

Some people purchase pre-printed invitations and add details about the time and place of the party, though sending out invitations online is becoming increasingly common. Other people make their own invitations, some of which are very fancy. More elaborate parties are announced with invitations printed on balloons, etched into slabs of chocolate, or engraved in pieces of wood. Whether an invitation is homemade or an expensive

Handmade birthday invitation created by Ava Acomba.
Shari Nakagawa

custom production, often its style reflects a particular theme chosen for the party.

Let's Eat!

Our family is not alone in our love of sharing tasty treats with friends! From noodles in Asia to pies in Russia, many foods, both sweet and savory, feature in birthday celebrations.

The preferred birthday breakfast treat in Ghana is *oto*, a patty made from mashed sweet potato and eggs, and fried in palm oil. Later in the day, stew, rice and *kelewele* (fried pieces of plantain) might be served.

China, Hong Kong and Korea are all places where serving extra-long noodles on someone's birthday is believed to be good luck. Long noodles represent a long life, so serving them is a way of saying you hope the birthday boy or girl will live for many more years.

Many places serve cake as part of the birthday menu. The modern birthday cake is most commonly attributed to the Germans and their celebration of Kinderfest, which recognized the birthdays of children. In the 1800s, German bakers realized that sweet cakes for children's birthday parties would be popular items. Luckily for those of us who love fancy cakes, these bakers started creating light, sweet cakes similar to those we know and enjoy today. Known as *Geburtstagstorten*, these cakes became more and more elaborate, tricky and time-consuming to make, until only the richest families could afford to buy them.

German cakes began to be topped with flaming candles during the eighteenth century. Instead of representing the light of the moon as they did in Ancient Greece (see page 16), each candle represented one year of the person's life, and one or more other candles were

Geburtstagstorten cakes can be incredibly colorful, intricate and large, just like this example.
SrdjanPav/iStock.com

Give It a Whirl!

Make a Birthday Calendar

You can make a birthday calendar by using twelve large index cards. At the top of each one print the name of a month. Decorate the edges of the card using stickers, felt pens or shapes cut out of colorful craft paper. Leave room at the top of each card to punch two holes. Thread a piece of ribbon through the holes to fasten the pages together. Write the name and birth date for every person you'd like to remember on the corresponding card. Each month, turn to a new card and see whose birthday is coming up next.

added to indicate the hope that the person would live a few more years as well. Today, some German families light one large candle (called a **Lebenskerze**, or **life candle**) and burn a part of that candle each year until the child turns 12.

The Lebenskerze is beautifully decorated and might be placed on a round disk (a **Geburstagskranz**), where additional smaller candles—one for each year—are lit around the Lebenskerze. Blowing out the birthday candles and then making a wish are common Western traditions. Usually, the wish is kept private, and it's said that the wish won't come true unless all the candles are blown out with one breath.

There's a good reason children in Germany bite into their cake gently: often a coin is baked into each piece. In medieval times in England, finding a coin in your cake

More people are born in August than any other month.

Phillip celebrates his tenth birthday with friends in Germany, with his Geburstagskranz at center stage.
Phillip Syvarth

was thought to be good luck and symbolized a wealthy future. In North America, it's less common to hide things inside a cake, but the outside is often covered with fancy decorations.

Because lots of friends and relatives are invited to birthday parties in Egypt, it's common to have two cakes, though only one has candles. Other snacks might include small individual cakes, sesame sticks and little sandwiches. All the food is served at the same time, and the house is decorated with paper garlands called *zeena* (which look a bit like chains of snowflakes).

Decorated cakes and pancakes sprinkled with powdered sugar are favorite treats when friends and family members in the Netherlands visit someone on their birthday. *Taartjes* (small tarts), served with lemonade or

If you celebrate your birthday in Germany, be careful when you bite into your cake! Coins are often tucked inside for someone lucky to find.
Shari Nakagawa

This Filipino birthday celebration features plenty of candies and other treats.
Erickson Floresca

In the Philippines, the seventh birthday is considered to be significant as it marks the transition from being a little kid to a school-age child who must start making responsible decisions. A girl celebrating her seventh birthday may wear a tiara and a spectacular dress.

hot chocolate, and *gebakjes* (small individual pastries) are more common than large birthday cakes with candles.

In the Philippines, the birthday cake (often decorated with a birthday message) might be served with a glass of Jaz, a cola-flavored soft drink found only in the Philippines. What else might be on the menu at a Filipino birthday party? How about *pancit* (long, thin noodles) and *lechon* (roast pork) or maybe *adobo* (chicken or pork and vegetables cooked with pineapple, vinegar, pepper, garlic and salt).

Ice cream is a popular party food in many places, but in Norway party guests have to go fishing for their frozen treats, which are hung from strings.

Birthday Gifts

In India, gifts are given on many occasions, but only some religious traditions include gift-giving for birthdays. It's considered bad form to wrap presents in black or white paper—bright colors are much preferred.

Rather than receiving many small gifts, it's common for a Swedish child to receive a very special present from the whole family, the type of gift one might treasure for a lifetime, like a very fancy watch or a piece of jewelry.

In Thailand, a child having a birthday may be given some live fish or birds, the number of creatures corresponding to the age of the child, plus one extra for good luck. The birthday child sprinkles special water on the animals and then sets them free, a gesture said to please the gods.

If you live in Finland, chances are you'll throw your birthday bash on the weekend. As guests arrive, they sing a birthday song at the door and offer gifts, which are opened as they are received.

While many of us enjoy receiving presents on our birthdays, in some places it's customary for guests at a birthday

Birthday Treats

You're Invited!

The very first birthday invitations may have been sent out as long ago as the first century CE. Messages written on very thin slices of wood were one way Romans occupying Great Britain communicated. One document, an invitation from Claudia Severa, a Roman commander's wife, invited Sulpicia Lepidena, a woman from a nearby fort, to come to a birthday party.

This engraved wooden invitation is a little bit fancier than invitations most people use for birthdays today, but is perfect for extra-special occasions.
Dani Tate-Stratton/skog.ca

Children in Sweden often receive *Dalahäst* (painted wooden horses) on their birthday.
iStock.com

party to receive a small gift as well. In Peru, there are two types of party favors: goody bags and souvenir pins made especially for the birthday party. Sometimes these pins are very fancy, and some Peruvian children collect them.

In India, dressy, colorful clothes are worn by the birthday child, who also kneels and touches his or her parents' feet to show respect. Visiting a shrine to pray and be blessed is another serious part of being a year older. Handing out chocolates is just plain fun. In the afternoon, the birthday meal might include spicy curry and chutney and *dudh pakh* for dessert. Dudh pakh is a bit like rice pudding with pistachios, almonds, raisins and a spice called cardamon (see recipe on page 39).

Give It a Whirl!

Pass the Parcel

One of our favorite party games is Pass the Parcel. If you want to play this game at a birthday party, you will need:

• A small gift to give to the winner of the game

• Many sheets of newspaper

• Music

How to Play

Before the guests arrive, wrap the small present in many layers of paper—at least one more layer of paper than the number of guests you expect to have at the party. When the guests are sitting in a circle, have one person (usually an adult who is not playing) start the music. When the music is playing, the guests should pass the parcel from one person to the next. Without warning, the person in charge of the music turns it off. Whoever is holding the package when the music stops removes one layer of paper. The music is started again, and the game continues until the lucky winner unwraps the last layer and keeps the gift inside!

Fun and Games

Piñatas are often made from papier-mâché, but can also be created from pottery or cloth.
Cathy Yeulet/iStock.com

Children in Mexico (and many other countries in Latin America, and in Europe) might celebrate with two parties on different days each year. On their saint's day (see page 18), the priest at the local church blesses the child, and the family has a party at home for relatives and close friends. On a Mexican child's actual birthday, lots of friends come over and take turns bashing at a *piñata*, a hollow paper container filled with candies and small treats. It's not easy to break open a piñata, as the children often wear a blindfold before taking a swing with a stick. Whenever someone is hitting a piñata, everyone around

Filipino children who are trying to get treats from a pabitin sometimes lift smaller children up to grab extra treats.
Chito Paner Images

them stands in a circle, claps their hands, and sings a special song, which begins, "*Dale, dale, dale. No pierdas el tino.*" ("Hit it, hit it, hit it. Don't lose your aim.")

In Ecuador, children often celebrate their saint's day with an afternoon tea party at which raisin cake, tea cookies and hot chocolate are common treats.

Birthdays and festivals in the Philippines often feature a *pabitin*, which is sort of like a Mexican piñata and is also made to hold candies, toys and fruit. The pabitin is raised while children gather underneath and wait for an adult to lower it. The children try to grab as many presents as possible before the pabitin is raised back out of reach. Sometimes children form teams and lift the smallest players up to take extra goodies.

Making the Birthday Person Feel Special

In many places, it's customary for the person celebrating the birthday to wear a special hat or fancy clothes.

There's no mistaking who is having the birthday in Israel. Just watch for the person wearing a crown of leaves or flowers. The birthday person will also be the one sitting in a chair decorated with streamers. Party guests dance around the chair and sing, and then present a cake shaped to represent the child's special interest. Everyone then enjoys races or games of skill, such as seeing who can run fastest while balancing a potato or a hard-boiled egg on a spoon.

Party decorations in Norway might include thin, colorful streamers and candies to decorate the table.

DUDH PAKH

Try this recipe for a birthday treat from India.

Ingredients

½ cup raisins

4 cups rice pudding (made from a mix or your favorite recipe)

1 tablespoon cardamom

1 teaspoon cinnamon

1 teaspoon allspice

½ cup slivered almonds

Directions

Soak the raisins in hot water for 10 minutes to soften them. Make the pudding according to directions. Stir the cardamon, cinnamon and allspice into the pudding. Drain the raisins. When the rice pudding has cooled, add raisins and half the almonds. Stir. Serve the pudding in party dishes. Decorate with the remaining almonds.

Birthday Treats

Giddyup!

One of the purposes of marking a birthday by hosting a special event is to make it memorable. One party in particular in my childhood stands out. When I turned 5 my family lived in Australia, and by that time I was already crazy about horses. My parents arranged to have a pony come to the party, and all the children who were invited took turns having pony rides. —NT

Colorful birthday garlands are an easy way to show you are celebrating a special day. *ruizluquepaz/iStock.com*

In Brazil, colorful candies shaped like fruits and vegetables and paper flowers are all common party decorations. The Netherlands is another country where decorations are important on a birthday. Garlands decorate the walls and garden of the house, as well as the birthday chair.

If you see someone walking down the street covered in flour, that's not always a sign the person is a messy baker. In Indonesia, celebrating a birthday might mean that your friends cover you in a mix of flour, water and eggs! That may seem like a mean way to help someone "celebrate," but it is actually a pretty convenient way to show it's your birthday! As soon as people see you walking around covered in flour, they are likely to wish you a *Selamat Ulang Tahun.*

Celebrating at School

Children in Russia are happy when their birthdays happen to fall on a school day, because it's quite common to receive small gifts (like pencils, flowers or books) from their teachers. Classmates might also offer small hand-made presents. Though birthdays are acknowledged at school, the big party usually takes place at home either after school or on the weekend.

A classroom in Sweden may also be the location for a birthday party, though the family of the birthday child is responsible for providing cake or ice cream. To honor the child, two people each hold an arm and a leg of the birthday child, who is then swung back and forth above the floor while everyone shouts, "Four times we

Birthday Treats

Bonus Birthday!

Because my birthday is in early January, the weather wasn't usually great and everyone was pretty tired of social gatherings so close to Christmas. As a child I often observed my *half birthday* in the summer instead. Several times, I chose to have a camping birthday party and spent a few hot days with close friends on the beaches not far from where we live on Vancouver Island. I still remember climbing huge trees, building driftwood forts and roasting marshmallows with my friends. —DTS

Dani (in pink shirt) celebrates her birthday up a tree.
Nikki Tate

honor you." This is similar to the birthday bumps given to children in North America when the child is lifted into the air and gently bumped against the ground, once for each year being celebrated.

Birthday Songs

There's no better way to start off a birthday than by waking up to a special song, which is what happens to the birthday child in Sweden. Family members sing,

He should live a hundred years,
He should live a hundred years,
Yes, I wish that he shall live to know a hundred years.

No matter how we choose to celebrate, sharing the special event of a birthday with people we care about is a wonderful way to mark the passage of time and make sure we create and share memories that will last a lifetime. In the next chapter, you'll see that some birthdays are thought to be extra special.

Friends sing "Happy Birthday" as this little boy blows out his birthday candles.
Rich Legg/iStock.com

Stevie's Story

Stevie celebrating at a pirate-themed birthday.
Duddy Family

A Birthday Down Under

Stevie Duddy grew up in Sydney, Australia, and throughout her childhood enjoyed birthday parties that involved "lots of games and food." Stevie says you can always tell where a birthday party is taking place in Australia, because the mailbox is brightly decorated with balloons and streamers. Games like Musical Chairs and Pin the Tail on the Donkey were popular at her parties. She also remembers taking advantage of the hot weather in Australia by hosting pool parties. In the water, Stevie and her friends played games like Marco Polo.

Food was often an outdoor affair as well. "It was common for the dads to help cook up a barbecue," Stevie says. "We would usually have sausages in bread with tomato sauce (ketchup), mini frankfurters and party pies, which are very small meat pies." A highlight of dessert was always "fairy bread," which is buttered white bread covered in a type of sprinkles known as *hundreds and thousands*. Stevie also remembers looking forward to a specially themed birthday cake, often picked from *The Australian Women's Weekly Birthday Cake Book*. "I usually got the maypole or the rabbit, and my brother usually got the soccer field."

As she was opening her gifts, her friends played Pass the Parcel until everyone got a present of their own, perhaps a yo-yo or Matchbox car. At the end of the party, everyone got to take home a party bag filled with mixed lollies (candy).

Stevie recalls that her eighteenth birthday was a very important one, partially because it was during her last year of secondary school. Like many of her friends, she celebrated during the evening with music and dancing at home.

Barbecue parties are very popular in Australia, where the weather is often ideal for an outdoor celebration.
iStock.com

Hoka's Story

Hoka remembers the older people in her life receiving birthday dumplings like these in Hong Kong.
Jui-Chi Chan/iStock.com

Delicious Dumplings and a Dutch Ditty

Hoka Wen, who currently lives in Ireland, moved around a lot as a child because of her father's job. One of her earliest birthday memories is from her family's time in Somalia. "The first birthday I can recall is my baby sister's. My mother made a cake, which she decorated with Lego people, because we were all pretty obsessed with Lego. Because at that time there were no bakers in Somalia who made birthday cakes or, as far as I know, even any cakes at all. Everything was homemade."

Another early birthday memory is of celebrating in Hong Kong, where Hoka's family is from. "Hong Kong was pretty English at that point, so kids' parties weren't particularly Chinese. I celebrated a birthday at McDonald's there when I turned 7." Hoka goes on to say that, in the Chinese tradition, children's birthdays aren't really celebrated. "It is the older folks who get the attention. We believe that the older you turn, the bigger your party, since at that point, it is more worth celebrating. Also, I have only seen Chinese birthday cakes at parties for older people. These cakes are sweet Chinese dumplings made to resemble peaches, with a bit of pink icing on top and filled with sweet bean paste. Peaches are symbolic of long life."

Hoka spent much of her childhood and young adult years in the Netherlands. One thing that stands out for her is that Dutch birthdays can go on for the whole day. "It's not really a party, but more like an open house where everyone drops by throughout the day to congratulate you and everybody else in the family." Hoka clearly remembers being congratulated for her sister's birthday as well as her own during one such event.

"If it's your birthday, it's usually your responsibility to ensure there is food and cake. This is more obvious when you get older and start working, because then you have to treat your coworkers to cake. As a kid, this often meant bringing snacks for everyone at school." Guests receive gifts for attending parties as well. "One year when I celebrated my birthday as a kid in Holland, my parents threw a circus-themed birthday party for me where every kid got to take home a mug filled with candy."

The Dutch birthday song is quite different from the one so common in North America. Hoka says, "We have a very old-fashioned one, which begins with 'Long will you live in glory.'" A second song is often sung at kids' parties and ends with the calling of "hip hip hooray" the same number of times as the birthday boy's or girl's age.

Hoka has a traditional Dutch milestone to look forward to. In Holland, when you turn 50, if you are a man it is said that you are "seeing Abraham," and if you are a woman, "seeing Sarah," in reference to the aged Biblical couple. Giant inflatable dolls adorning your front yard go along with the saying, which refers to the fact that you are half a century old. *Gelukkige verjaardag*, Hoka!

Candy in a mug, similar to this one, was given by Hoka to all of her guests at one Dutch birthday party. *ClaudioVentrella/iStock.com*

Birthday Treats

Happy Birthday to You!

One of the best known songs in the world is "Happy Birthday to You!" Translated into at least eighteen languages, the famous song is believed to have been first sung in the late 1800s in a kindergarten class taught by Patty Hill. Patty and her sister Mildred originally used the words "Good morning to all" but changed the words to "Happy Birthday to you!" Eventually, this became the version that is so well known today.

A young boy is helped through his bar mitzvah at the Western Wall in Jerusalem. One of the holiest sites in Judaism, it has been used for prayer since at least the sixteenth century. Today, there are organizations that support Jewish children from all around the world and help them become bar or bat mitzvahs at this important spot.
RobertHoetink/iStock.com

THREE

MILESTONE BIRTHDAYS

Turning a year older is a momentous occasion every time it happens, but in many cultures there are specific ages that are cause for even *more* celebration, respect or attention than others. In some places, surviving infancy is worthy of special recognition, while elsewhere becoming an adult or reaching a very senior birthday is considered to be an especially good reason to throw a party.

Welcome, Baby!

The day a new baby arrives is always special. In Ethiopia, people shout out the news of a baby being born. If the baby is a girl, then it's customary to call out three times. If the baby is a boy, expect to hear a rousing chorus of five shouts.

After you turn 60 in China, birthdays are typically observed only every tenth year, which is a long time to wait between parties!

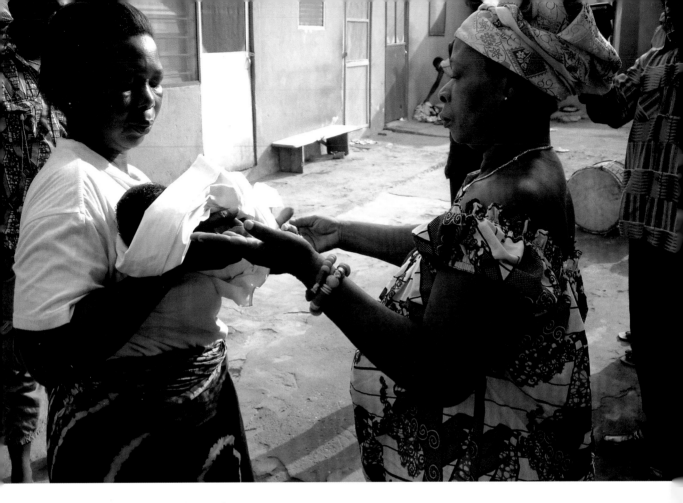

This new baby is "outdooring," or meeting the members of its community.
Easy Track Ghana, Ltd.

In West Africa, when a baby is 8 days old, it's time for **outdooring**. The new arrival in the community is taken outside to see the world and meet friends and family.

In Egypt, a similar custom is observed on a baby's seventh day. Children in the community lead a parade and sing a special song:

> *Birgalatak, Birgalatak,*
> *Golden earrings brightly dangling,*
> *O God bless him, may he grow up*
> *And run hither, and play thither*
> *Up and down the house all over.*
> *Birgalatak, Birgalatak!*

Alive and Well and Ready to Celebrate

While the birth of a baby is very exciting, in areas where babies often die soon after birth, parents wait until the child has survived the highest-risk period of an infant's early life before fully celebrating the arrival of the newest family member.

Some ceremonies are designed to protect the baby as it passes through the first, delicate stages of life. One such event is the baby-jumping festival held annually in Castrillo de Murcia, Spain. On the day known as El Salto del Colacho (the Devil's Jump), newborn babies are placed on mattresses on the street and sprinkled with confetti. Local men dressed up like devils then leap over the babies! This ritual, which is said to date back to 1620, is meant to

Birthday Treats

New Year Baby

The first baby born in a community on January 1 is often treated like a celebrity, receiving gifts and appearing in the local media. A child who arrives on January 1 is said to bring good luck to his or her family throughout the coming year. As far back as the Ancient Greeks, people have considered a new baby to be a symbol of a new start, and it's still common for an image of a baby to be used to represent the beginning of a new year.

Don't trip! Baby jumping, a custom unique to Castillo de Murcia, Spain, cleanses bad spirits from the community.
Wikipedia

cleanse both the babies and the town alike, and protect the children from evil spirits in the future.

In traditional Chinese families, it is still customary for a new mother to stay in relative isolation for a full month after the birth of her baby. This allows her to recover from birth, get to know the new child, and limit exposure to germs and well-meaning but intrusive friends and family members. To mark the end of this period, there is a "full moon" or "full month" celebration, at which the extended family meets the new child for the first time and everyone celebrates the health of the baby by performing certain rituals. Red eggs, said to symbolize fertility, are often served along with traditional rice cakes and pickled red ginger. Visitors bring gifts for the new mother and her baby. Traditionally, money or jewelry were common gifts, but clothing and toys are becoming more popular.

Red eggs symbolize fertility in China and are often served when a baby turns 1 month old.
Marccophoto/iStock.com

In Korea, reaching 100 days of age is a happy event worth marking. It's believed that if a family shares steamed rice cakes with a hundred friends and family members around the time of a child's one-hundredth day, the child will live for many years. Well-wishers fill the same containers the family used for the rice cakes with thread and rice and give them back as a way of sharing their hope that the child will have a long and prosperous life. If a child has been sick, then the one-hundredth day is not observed at all, to avoid bringing more bad luck.

This Korean baby is dressed up in traditional clothing to celebrate its first birthday, the next major milestone after one hundred days. *Wikipedia*

That's One Big Party!

You might think there is only one way to keep track of someone's age, but it turns out different cultures keep track of birthdays in different ways. Traditionally,

Birthday Treats

Star Birthday

Sometimes a birthday is special because of the date on which it happens. Known as "champagne," "golden," "lucky" or "star" birthdays, these extra-special days are when you turn the age that corresponds to your birth date. For example, if you were born on the fifteenth of the month, your star birthday would happen when you turn 15.

Depending which item this toddler grabs first, his Korean family may see it as a glimpse into his future.
Ginaellen/Dreamstime.com

countries such as China, Japan, Vietnam and Korea used a single date (February 4 or 5) on which all people born in a given year became a year older. In Korea, most people still calculate their age based on a shared birthday, though a person's actual date of birth is used on legal documents. Today, most Asian countries have adopted the custom of calculating age based on an individual's date of birth rather than by using a single universal birthday.

When to start counting is also less straightforward than you might expect. In many places, a child turns 1 a year after he or she was born. But in China, Vietnam and Korea, a newborn is 1 and at twelve months, turns 2. This system is called ***East Asian age reckoning***.

Say Goodbye to the Past

In cultures in which people believe in **reincarnation** (the idea that after someone dies that person's soul is reborn into a new body), a ceremony may be held to help the child complete the most recent past life and fully transition into the current body.

Buddhist monks in Thailand shave a baby's head one month and a day after birth. This ritual is said to purify the baby of any ill effects that might be caused by lingering spirits.

Mongolians also observe an important hair-cutting rite when little girls turn 2 and boys turn 3. The ceremony shows that the child has become a toddler and is no longer considered a baby. In Mongolian culture, babies are in a place of transition between our world and the world of spirits, and this ceremony signifies that they have fully entered our world.

What Does the Future Hold?

Attempting to tell the future is part of the *doljanchi* celebration held when a baby in Korea reaches 1 year of age. Various items (such as a book, food, money or thread) are placed on a table in front of the child. The child chooses an item, and it's thought that this selection foretells their future. A baby who chooses food will never be hungry and one who selects money will be wealthy.

Families in Turkey try to influence the future by using a baby's umbilical cord. It is said that the location in which the umbilical cord is buried will influence future

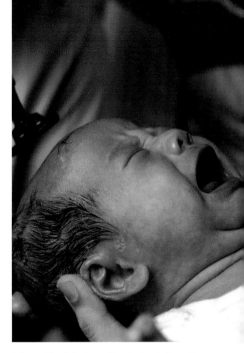

A 1-month-old baby getting its head shaved by a Buddhist monk in Thailand.
Khunaspix/Dreamstime.com

The oldest woman on record is Jeanne Calment (1875–1997) from France, who lived to the age of 122 years, 164 days. The oldest living man was Jiroemon Kiumra of Japan (1897–2013), who died at age 116 years, 54 days. Imagine living through the invention of light bulbs, radios, cars, planes, televisions, computers and self-driving cars!

job prospects. Burying the cord by a stable could turn the child into an animal lover, but a burial location near the library might result in the child becoming a professor or an author. For those who don't want to interfere, throwing the cord into water is said to leave the future entirely up to chance.

Coming of Age

In many cultures, certain ages signify children are growing up. Often a special ritual marks the transition from child to adult.

In North America you can drive at one age, drink alcohol at another, and join the military and vote at yet another. In Japan, all of those milestone events happen together on the day you turn 20. Twenty is such an important age that a national holiday is held in January in honor of people who will turn 20 that year. On *Seijin no Hi* (Adult's Day), young women dress up in brightly colored fancy kimonos (young men usually wear suits and ties) and attend a special gathering with politicians and performers at the local *kuyakusho* (town hall). After that, young adults perform various rituals at their neighborhood shrine as a way to help ensure a bright and successful future. While families also attend those two events, the evening is often reserved for friends to celebrate together.

Sometimes becoming an adult is celebrated with huge parties attended by friends and family. In the Jewish faith, bar and bat mitzvahs take place when girls turn 12 and boys turn 13 years old, although these celebrations are not religious requirements. At those ages, children are ready to take responsibility for their actions and become

In Great Britain before good dental care was common, some people had all their teeth pulled out and were given a set of dentures as a special twenty-first birthday present. Though that might not sound like a great present, having false teeth saved on dental bills later in life.

Adult's Day is an opportunity for Japanese childhood friends to reconnect.
John Leung/Shutterstock.com

full-fledged members of the Jewish community. A bat or bar mitzvah is usually a two-part event. During a ceremony at the synogogue, the child reads from the Torah (the main religious text of the Jewish faith) and gives a special blessing. Depending on the community, the child might learn long passages of Hebrew to recite and will often give a speech. It takes months of learning and preparation to get ready for a bar or bat mitzvah. After the ceremony it's time for friends and family to celebrate! Just like weddings, some bar and bat mitzvah parties are small and others are huge and dramatic, and may cost many thousands of dollars.

In Muslim communities in Malaysia, some girls spend years preparing for **Khatam Al Koran**, a ceremony that

This girl is reading from the Torah as part of her bat mitzvah celebrations.
Shutterstock.com

Malaysian girls show their maturity through preparations for a ceremony known as Khatam Al Koran.
Amar Syafiq

occurs when they are about to turn 11. To show their maturity as young Muslim women, the girls are expected to recite passages from the Koran (the main religious text of the Muslim faith) to everyone at the mosque. Many girls take special classes in recitation to prepare. After the solemn religious service a picnic at the beach with family is one way in which this special day is observed.

Another party marking the transition to adulthood is the *quinceañera*, which is a popular Latin American celebration for girls turning 15 (in Spanish, *quince* means fifteen, *año* means year). These social gatherings present the young woman to the community, at the same time showing she is an adult. Girls often choose a "court of honor," which is made up of the people closest to her (and of similar age). They might be friends, sisters, brothers or cousins, who are often dressed formally, in ball gowns or tuxedos.

By changing his daughter's shoes, this father is acknowledging her transition from girl to woman.
William Steen

In Denmark a Danish flag flies outside the house so everyone knows a birthday is being celebrated.

One of the traditions in a Mexican quinceañera is the **Changing of the Shoes**. A favorite male relative (the girl's father or an uncle) helps her change from flat shoes to heels, which symbolizes her transition from girl to woman.

When a girl turns 15 in Uruguay, she puts on a fancy dress and dances a waltz with various young men, who are considered to be possible future marriage partners.

Growing Up Can Be Painful

Becoming an adult is not all fun and parties though. For the Sateré Mawé tribe in Brazil, part of coming of age (in this case at around 12 or 13) is proving your readiness as a warrior. If you wish to join the ranks of the elders, you must show that you have a high pain tolerance, which is tested with a unique ritual involving ants.

Paraponera clavata, or bullet ants, which pack an amazing punch with their sting, are found in the Amazon near where this group lives. Not only does the initial sting burn, but the toxins the ants inject also interfere with the human central nervous system, leading to shaking, pain and other effects that can last for several days. Something you would want to avoid at all costs, right? Not so for the young Sateré Mawé warriors. Elder tribesmen sedate and collect many of the venomous creatures and then weave them—stingers facing in—into a pair of gloves, which the young boys wear for about ten minutes.

The boys are stung repeatedly, but they endure the pain while trying not to cry out, which is all part of showing their readiness to become warriors. Elder members of the tribe sing and dance to distract them from the pain, but ultimately the boys must find ways to endure the pain, paralysis and hallucinations. In order to become full-fledged warriors, this coming-of-age ceremony may be performed as many as twenty times!

Don't Lose Your Key!

In England, to acknowledge that their child has become an adult, some families give him or her a key to the house when the child turns 21. A symbol of both freedom and responsibility, the key traditionally meant the young adult could then stay out of the house as late as he or she wanted to. There's even a song from 1912 called "I'm 21 Today," which goes (in part):

I'm 21 today, 21 today
I've got the key of the door

Birthday Treats

Out of This World!

It can be tricky to organize a party for someone who is traveling on their birthday. Astronaut Leland Melvin couldn't have been much farther away from home when he turned 44! He was orbiting around Earth on the space shuttle *Atlantis* while it was linked to the International Space Station, but that didn't stop his family from throwing a party. Using video cameras, Melvin was able to chat with friends and family even though he was floating around in space. "My baby sister always surprises me with crazy parties," he admitted. "This has to top them all."

Never been 21 before
And Pa says I can do as I like
So shout, Hip Hip Hooray
He's a jolly good fellow
21 today.

Time to Tidy Up!

If you are a single man turning 30 in Germany, there may be some public housework in your future! Tradition says a single young man should sweep the steps of the city hall. Helpful friends even gather to throw dirt, confetti, bottle caps and other hard-to-sweep items onto the stairs to give him more to do! This is supposed to be a bit embarrassing, but mostly funny, and stops only once the young man kisses an unmarried girl who happens to be passing by. The reason for this spontaneous house-work, known as *Treppe fegen oder Klinken putzen*, is an old belief that once in the afterlife, unmarried men would be forced to do boring odd jobs.

Birthday Treats

A Letter from the Queen

In the Queen of England's Commonwealth realms and British Overseas Territories, citizens can apply for and receive a personalized congratulatory letter from the Queen for their 100th and 105th birthday, and then each year thereafter.

Not quite 100? Not to worry. Other heads of state might be willing to send a letter to a younger citizen. When Dani's grandfather turned 80, she filled out an online form through the Office of the Prime Minister of Canada. The day before she threw a big birthday party for her grandfather, a very nice certificate signed by Prime Minister Justin Trudeau arrived in the mail! She had it framed, and the official letter certainly added an air of formality to the event. —NT

Grampa was excited by both the surprise party we threw him and the certificate, which was a highlight of the already-special occasion.
Dani Tate-Stratton

Sweeping the steps of the city hall is a funny tradition still carried out in Germany.
Volker Wurst

The tradition for unmarried women in Germany is similar. When they reach the age of 30, they must polish all of the door handles of the town until an unmarried man frees them with a kiss. This tradition represents a woman polishing the door handle of a convent (a Christian religious community for nuns) to ask for entrance. In the past, a common assumption was that an older woman would never marry and would have no choice but to dedicate her life to religious work. Today, it is quite normal for adults of any age to marry, but the tradition of polishing door handles is still sometimes practiced for fun.

Respecting Your Elders

People reaching their senior years can look forward to all sorts of important rituals and parties that recognize their long lives. Some celebrations also commemorate and honor a person's commitment to society over a lifetime.

In China, one of the most significant ages is 60. It is believed that by this point a person has lived through one

Miyeok-guk Soup

In Korea, it is so common to eat this seaweed soup on your birthday that instead of wishing you a "Happy Birthday," people might ask you, "Have you had miyeok-guk?" Also eaten by moms who have just given birth, this soup is a warm, comforting and extremely healthy way to salute your special day. It is traditionally served with rice, which is added to the soup a little bit at a time just before eating each spoonful.

Ingredients:

1 cup dried *miyeok* (dried seaweed, which may also be labeled as *wakame*)

16 cups water

8 ounces beef brisket

1 tablespoon minced garlic

4–5 tablespoons fish sauce

2 tablespoons sesame oil

Cooked rice for serving

Directions:

Cut or rip the seaweed into small pieces (1 or 2 inches square) and then put them into a large bowl and cover with 4 cups of the water. Soak for 30 minutes, stir, and leave for another 30 minutes. This should result in approximately 4 cups of seaweed. Add the seaweed to a large pot and cover with the rest of the water. Over high heat and with the pot lid partly on, boil for 20 minutes. While the soup is boiling, cut the beef brisket into bite-size pieces. Reduce heat to medium. Carefully add beef and garlic to the soup, and boil for another 20–25 minutes. Add the fish sauce and drizzle the sesame oil into the soup just before serving.

complete life cycle (based on an astrological system that combines the twelve signs of the zodiac with five natural elements: metal, fire, water, earth and wood). A sixtieth birthday celebration might include eating noodles and peaches to signify a long life, getting together with friends and family, and receiving money, flowers and cakes.

In Korea, the traditional age to celebrate an older birthday was always 60. Since few people used to live this long, reaching your *hwanggap* (sixtieth birthday) was a major accomplishment to be lavishly celebrated by friends and family. Now, however, longer life expectancy is giving rise to the *gohui/chilsun* (seventieth birthday) and *palsun* (eightieth birthday).

No matter which specific decade is recognized, the festivities are similar. Family members and the person celebrating a birthday often dress up in *hanbok*,

The older you are in China, the more important your birthday. Generations of family celebrate with this elderly man. *iStock.com*

Birthday Treats

Happy Fiftieth!

For my fiftieth birthday party bash, Dani found two photos from each decade of my life. She printed them, labeled them and placed them in frames so party guests could enjoy them and get a glimpse into different chapters of my life story. Printed photos might be going out of style, but maybe at a future party we will arrange to have a slideshow running on a computer or send copies of the images to all our guests. Sharing photos in any format is a great way to bring back memories! —NT

Horse racing often plays a part in celebrating birthdays in Mongolia, where the birthday person presents a special scarf to the winner.
Bridgeman Images

traditional Korean clothing. Certain special foods, including meats, fish, rice cakes and pastries, are piled up high. Often the oldest son brings wine, presenting it as a gift to his parent and pouring their glass first.

The same person (or sometimes a group of friends and family members) brings a poem, message or song to read or perform in honor of the parent. While it isn't as common nowadays, adult children sometimes dress up as babies or young children and sing children's songs to make their aging parents feel younger.

In Mongolia, when you turn 61, 73, or 85, your family is expected to hold a birthday celebration and banquet in your honor. The festivities include a small competition featuring wrestling, horse racing and horse catching. While the birthday person does not necessarily ride in the games, they present a blessing *hada* (long silk scarf) to the winner.

Often celebratory fermented mare's milk and other dairy products are served during the festivities. In Mongolia, the birthday party is considered not only a way to mark the actual birthday but also an opportunity to take note of the contributions the person has made toward Mongolia over the course of a lifetime.

Kemberling Ochoa presents a bouquet of flowers to Our Lady of Guadalupe after the Catholic mass marking the beginning of her quinceañera festivities.
William Steen

Ana's Story

Twins, Treats, and Truth or Dare

Ana grew up with her twin sister in the small European country of Slovenia and loved celebrating her birthday with her twin. "It is always so nice to celebrate together, especially because we share the same group of friends. On our birthday we realize even more how close we are, how we share everything in our lives, including our birth date. So far we have spent three birthdays apart, and those years I missed her a lot."

For Ana, childhood birthday parties usually involved homemade treats, including sweets brought to school to share during the lunch break. For celebrations outside of school, Ana says, "We would write invitations for the birthday party and hand them out to the school friends that were invited. The party usually took place at our home, where we would gather in one of the rooms and play different games, like Truth or Dare, or something equally silly. Everyone brought a small gift and there were usually balloons." Along with chips and sandwiches, often a homemade birthday cake and candles were part of the celebration, as was the singing of "*Vse najboljše*," the Slovenian "Happy Birthday" song.

Whenever possible, Ana and her twin sister, Živa, have always tried to celebrate their birthdays together. Here they are as 2-year-olds at home in Slovenia.
Mojca Vodušek

Because her birthday is in February, Ana sometimes celebrated it later in the year to take advantage of better weather: "For two of my birthday parties I invited my friends to celebrate with me in June. I invited them to a big pool in the city, where we swam and had a lot of fun on the water slides. In the late afternoon we went to my home where we had a cake."

As with Stevie (see page 44), the most important birthday Ana has celebrated so far is her eighteenth, which in Slovenia is when you are considered an adult, with new responsibilites and freedoms. Ana celebrated her eighteenth birthday out of town with her twin and friends. "We invited all of our friends to a cabin we rented near the city, bought a lot of refreshments, and got a good sound system. We played the music we loved and danced all night."

A birthday celebration at the waterslides.
Henrique NDR Martins/iStock.com

Dani's Story

Dani wears a gorgeous kimono on Adult's Day in Japan.
Peter Williams

The year I turned 20, I happened to be living in Japan and was lucky enough to take part in Adult's Day. My aunt rented me a beautiful *furosode*, a formal kimono. With bright colors and sleeves so long they almost reached the ground, it indicated that I was young, unmarried and celebrating. A fancy white (fake) fur shawl made the kimono winter-appropriate. (Eating while wearing the kimono was very stressful! I've never worn such expensive clothing, not even on my wedding day.)

Because formal kimonos are handwoven from silk, no two are exactly alike, and they can be incredibly expensive, often costing many thousands of dollars. Kimonos, and the intricate *obi* (belts) worn with them, are not easy to put on, so along with the rental came a booking at a special kimono dressing salon. First my hair and makeup were done, and then three different women came to help me dress, a process that took several hours.

After the function at our local city hall, it was time for a trip to Meiji Jingu Shrine, where we joined hundreds of new adults in performing rituals for a successful new year. We wrote our wishes on a piece of wood to hang at the shrine, and purchased decorative wooden arrows to put at the head of our beds to ward off bad spirits.

It was an incredible day and one that I remember every January. What a fantastic way to begin life as an adult!

Dani on Adult's Day.
Peter Williams

Nikki and Dani near their home in Victoria, BC.
Nichole Taylor Photography

A final word from the authors

Writing this book was a fantastic chance for us to reflect on the important birthdays we've enjoyed and to learn more about how our friends, family members and ancient ancestors celebrate. It was exciting to recognize connections between ancient rituals and the traditions we take for granted today. Interviewing our friends from around the world reminded us of the rich variation in people's life experiences. At the same time it was reassuring to see all the similarities so many of us share when it comes to celebrating a long life well-lived. We are taking away many ideas for future celebrations and hope you've discovered something new to incorporate into your next birthday as well!

A note from the series editor

"The Origins are built on the bedrock of personal stories, enhanced by careful research and illuminated by stunning photographs. No book can be all things to all people, and no two people experience a culture in the same way. The Origins are not meant to be the definitive word on any culture or belief; instead they will lead readers toward a place where differences are acknowledged and knowledge facilitates understanding."

—Sarah N. Harvey

GLOSSARY

astrology—a study of the positions and relationships of the sun, moon, stars and planets in order to judge their influence on human actions

baptism—a Christian ceremony marked by ritual use of water and admitting the recipient to the Christian community

birthday calendar—a book or calendar that lists important birth dates by date rather than day of the week so that the list can be used again year after year

Changing of the Shoes—a ceremony on a girl's fifteenth birthday, particularly in Mexico, in which the birthday girl's shoes are changed from flats to heels to symbolize her transition from girl to woman, as part of the Latin American quinceañera celebration

coronation—the ceremony in which a crown is placed on the head of a new king or queen to symbolize their power as monarch

decans—an Ancient Egyptian system of marking time by tracking the stars in the sky on ten-day cycles

East Asian age reckoning—a way of counting age that originated in China and is widely used by other cultures in East Asia in which newborns start at the age of 1 for their first year and turn 2 after twelve months

Geburstagkranz—a candle wreath centerpiece

half birthday—the date approximately six months from your actual birthday

Industrial Revolution—the transition to new manufacturing processes that involved replacing human labor with machines (from 1760 to sometime between 1820 and 1840)

Khatam Al Koran—a ceremony in Malaysia in which Muslim girls turning 11 recite passages from the Koran to show their maturity as young Muslim women

leaper or **leapling**—someone born on February 29 of a leap year

leap year—a year, occurring once every four years, that has 366 days and includes February 29 on the calendar

Lebenskerze or **life candle**—a tall candle that some German families light and burn a part of each year until a child turns 12

name days—a day of celebration based on saint's days for anyone sharing a name with that particular saint

outdooring—a tradition in Ethiopia where a new baby is taken outside to see the world and meet friends and family on his or her eighth day of life

pagan—the name Christians give to anyone who believes in a religion other than Christianity

pharaoh—the name for a king in Ancient Egypt

reincarnation—the idea that after someone dies that person's soul is reborn into a new body

Renaissance—a time of cultural rebirth that took place in Europe between about 1300 and 1700 CE

zodiac—an imaginary area in the sky that the sun, moon and planets appear to travel through, which is divided into twelve star groups that have special names and symbols associated with each

REFERENCES AND RESOURCES

Chapter One

Books:

Forrester, Tina, and Sheryl Shapiro. *The Birthday Book*. Illustrated by Suzane Langlois. Annick Press, 2003.

Websites:

About News: The Origins of the Chinese Zodiac. www.chineseculture.about.com/od/chinesesuperstitions/a/Chinesezodiac.htm

Ancient Egypt Online. www.ancientegyptonline.co.uk/index.html

History Net: When Did People Start Celebrating Birthdays? www.historynet.com/when-did-people-start-celebrating-birthdays.htm

Chapter Two

Books:

Ichikawa, Satomi, and Elizabeth Laird. *Happy Birthday! A Book of Birthday Celebrations*. Collins, 1987.

Ingalls, Ann. *Birthday Traditions Around the World* (World Traditions). Illutrated by Elisa Chavarri. Child's World, 2013.

Lankford, Mary D. *Birthdays Around the World*. Illustrated by Karen Dugan. Harper Collins, 2002.

Powell, Jillian. *A Birthday* (*Why Is This Day Special?*). Smart Apple Media, 2007.

Websites:

BirthdayCelebrations.Net: Happy Birthday. www.birthdaycelebrations.net/favorites.htm

Parents: Birthday Party Theme Ideas for Kids 9 and Up. www.parents.com/fun/birthdays/themes/birthday-party-theme-ideas-kids-9-up/

Chapter Three

Books:

Kring, Robin. Memorable *Milestone Birthdays: 48 Theme Parties to Help You Celebrate*.
    Meadowbrook, 2001.

Websites:

iWonder: How are new babies celebrated around the world? www.bbc.co.uk/guides/zysbcdm

Global Citizen: 13 amazing coming of age traditions from around the world. www.globalcitizen.org
    /en/content/13-amazing-coming-of-age-traditions-from-around-th/

INDEX

*Page numbers in **bold** indicate an image; there may also be text related to the same topic on that page*

Acknowledgments

Finding a great collaborator is tough, but it's been a pleasure to work on another book project with my daughter, Dani (our first was *Take Shelter* in the Orca Footprints series). As always, the midwife team at Orca Book Publishers has been fantastic as this book has been birthed! Sarah Harvey's wise editorial guidance, Rachel Page's lovely design and the stellar teams in marketing and promotion have helped *Birthdays* along at every step. Many thanks to those who contributed their birthday experiences, photographs and encouragement. Without your help, this book would not have been possible. —NT

As always, many thanks to my co-author and mom, Nikki—at this point I can't imagine doing one of these on my own, so you are stuck with me now! Toryn, you continue to be my "prince of a guy." I am so very lucky to have you in my corner. Thank you. And of course, a huge thank-you to everyone at Orca! I'm so lucky to be supported by such an amazing Canadian house. Sarah Harvey's gentle but always spot-on guidance toward clarity and coherence is extremely appreciated (especially after the rewrites are complete!), and I am so in love with Rachel Page's design. To so many others behind the scenes, thank you so much for all you do to support Canadian publishing. I know my thanks are echoed by many. —DTS

Orca Origins

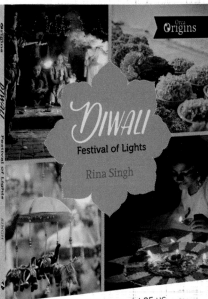